KU-332-026

目录
CONTENTS

七年之痒

文：艾未未

过去七年，夏星每年做一件作品，这件作品大约由60幅油画构成，每幅涉及一张新闻照片，一副忠实于原照的临摹。

绘画称为一个去个人化的过程，夏星在绘制过程中会做极少的技巧处理，他做过尺寸上统一的调整，和画法处理方式的微小的改变，比如说09、10年是采用单色的多次覆层的处理，黄颜色画一遍，红颜色罩一遍，蓝颜色罩一遍，像早期彩色电视分色一样的呈现图像。那更是一个技术程式和监控的方法。在这里他要画什么不由他决定，是由传媒和当天发生的事件构成，下一张图是什么，具有内容上的不确定性。

他的做法包含了多层的含义，一个就是画面的主题性、绘画性、语言探讨，诸如传统绘画的继承价值已不再是他的兴趣所在，不在他的日常绘画活动的工作范围中，就像一个终身的守夜打更人一样，守夜打更本身只是他度过的一种方式。

当一种行为被持续延续，支撑它的逻辑是什么，为什么它是其他行为方式不可替代的，如此行为始终在说，绘制从一个平面的介质，有如报纸，是一个被反复着的媒介，经过了编辑、选择，和重新绘制的时候，这种行为反复呈现以一年的众多图像作为一个作品的时候，它又会是一个什么样的表达，这个问题并不是其他的艺术家所涉及的。艺术提出了一个重要问题，它的形式，不管对它是如何评判，即使到再没有评判的余地的时候，它仍然是具有特征的。夏星的画作既无开始，也没有结束，像是一辆在行驶中的长途汽车，人们不再关心这辆车到底会在哪里停下，无论上车还是下车，车会一直在运行，你上车，然后继续前行。

绘画活动很多时候是一种逃避，这只是很小的一个层面，因为逃避没有涉及到公共存在的理由。什么叫绝对化，就是抓个什么东西就能画了。逃避本身是一种力量，这种力量产生和存在于大多数人的本身的能力，已经成为了潜意识的一部分。我们看不到真正的堕落、腐败或者是怯懦，或者是说真正的逃避，在这个世界上呆过一段时间后。没有真正的了不起的堕落存在，大家都非常一般。一般化是艺术里比较严重而通常的问题，解释成为多余，没有存在的必要了。

自2004年以来，夏星一共完成了7件作品，这样的一组油画，画面的尺寸在一年当中不变，最初是70厘米乘100厘米，07、08年变为140厘米乘200厘米，09年后成为35厘米乘50厘米。所绘内容皆是对同时期的同一家报纸的新闻摄影图片的重现，新闻里出现什么，夏星就画些什么，他几乎每天画画，五年中画了四百多张。确切地说，夏星这些年在用同一种方式画同一件作品，只是在等待下一张的新闻图片的出现，绘画是持续的等待，什么时候会完他自己也不知道。

在这一系列绘画中，没有自我构图取舍，极少对图片裁剪。它们大多是彩色的，是封面或是封内的图片，每年有些许不同关注，07他对与儿童有关题材更有兴趣，09年的，用他的话，则是关注"民间的生存方式"，2010年都是选择了关于维权的画面。

作为具有政治立场的绘画和相关的绘画性问题，在这里的人们总是回避或否认。在大多的情形下，这片土地上最为擅长的艺术仅仅是装腔作势、无病呻吟，或是谄媚巧淫的虚假制作，人们早已不敢正视现实，没有勇气觉察到周围每天发生的事件。在一个文化沦陷之地，文学艺术总会是腐败和懦弱的最好的样本。

言说事实是有必要的，言说的可能性永远会存在，这大概是绘画依然存在的重要的理由。

在穿越中国当代艺术的虚伪繁华的废墟之后，今天的艺术，仍然可以是帮助我们正视这个时代的面目和内心的可能。这个时代必然会成为过去，这个时代的羞辱和衰败必然会忠实的存活在这些画面的笔触中。

2011.3.23

The Seven-Year Itch

by Ai Weiwei

For the last seven years, Xia Xing has created one work per year. Each work consists of about 60 oil paintings, and each individual painting is a reproduction of one of the news photos he has chosen to paint.

Painting is said to proceed from a process of depersonalization, and Xia Xing uses the least possible treatment in terms of technique. He has adjusted his images to produce a uniform size and has brought some minute alterations to his painting technique. For example, in 2009 and 2010 he adopted a monochrome treatment with multiple coatings, painting a yellow layer, and then superimposing a red layer, followed by a blue one, in a manner reminiscent of the color separation of early color TV images. This is a method of "programming" the colors and monitoring their application. What Xia Xing paints is not determined by him, but rather is dictated by the media and current events, and the content of the next image is thus always up in the air.

His methods encompass many levels of meaning, including painting's subjects, style and the diction of discourse. Subjects such as the legacy of traditional painting's values are no longer of interest to him, since they fall well beyond the perimeter of his daily painting activities and work. Xia Xing seems condemned to a lifetime vigil as a night watchman, spending his life making his nocturnal rounds.

What, then, is the logic supporting this continuously drawn-out activity? Why doesn't some other form of behavior come along to supplant it? Acting in this way (to recap) is to draw from a flat medium such as newsprint - itself a repetitive medium – that then undergoes the processes of editing, selection and being repainted. And when this repetitive behavior culminates in one year's mass of images being transformed into a work, just what kind of expression is this supposed to be? This is not the sort of question that preoccupies other artists. Yet art does pose an important question. Its form, however judged - even if there has been no way to judge it at the time in question - still possesses certain features. In Xia Xing's case, his paintings have neither beginning nor end. They suggest a long-distance bus in motion, when the people on board have ceased to care where the bus will stop. Whether you get on or off, the bus is always moving. So you just get on the bus, and then you continue onward.

Acts of painting are very often an escape, but this is merely one very small aspect. The notion of escape finds no place within the rationale for public life. What is an absolute, however, is something that you can grasp hold of and then paint. Escape is itself a force generated by and present in most people's capacity, and one already embedded in their subconscious. We cannot truly perceive depravity, corruption and cowardice, or see a real escape route after we have spent some time in this world. There is no grandeur in the existence of depravity; everyone becomes very ordinary. Ordinariness is a relatively egregious but common problem in our art, which is deemed superfluous even when trying to explain what it is, and therefore lacks any real need to continue existing.

Since 2004, Xia Xing has created seven works of this kind of agglomerative painting, the size of whose individual units does not change within any one year. This was initially 70 x 100 cm, but this changed to 140 x 200 in 2007 and 2008, becoming 35 x 50 cm after 2009. Painted content is all reproduced from photo images appearing in the same newspaper in the same period, so that whatever appears in the news is what Xia Xing paints. He paints almost every day, and has amassed more than 400 paintings in five years. To state it more incisively, Xia Xing, using the same method for one full year to produce one work, is always awaiting the appearance of the next news photo, so his painting is a regimen of constant waiting, with even he himself unaware of when a work may be finished.

There is no room for personal choice in composing these serial works, and so very few of these photos are trimmed or cropped. Most are in color and taken from the front page or the first few pages of the newspaper. Each year has a somewhat different focus. In 2007, Xia Xing was more interested in materials relating to children. In 2009, he changed his focus to, in his words, "the civil way of life", while in 2010 his paintings all dealt with the protection of rights.

In relation to paintings that adopt a political stance (and address associated issues related to painting), people often stand in a perpetual state of evasion or denial. In the majority of cases, the most accomplished art in our patch of land serves merely to kick up a fuss, posture or throw fits of hypochondriac languor, or it produces vainglory that panders to sycophancy and sensual desire. People have for too long not dared to see reality. They lack the gumption to observe what is happening all around them every day. In our land of fallen culture, literature and art always necessarily present the best examples of corruption and cowardice.

To speak truth is a need. The possibility of speech will always persist. This is probably a major reason why painting still survives. After we have traversed the rubble of Chinese contemporary art's period of hypocritical prosperity, today's art will continue to guide us in viewing this era in its true light and seeing its intrinsic possibilities. This era must ineluctably fade into the past, but the humiliation and decline of our age will inevitably and faithfully live on, enshrined in the brush strokes of these paintings.

March 23, 2011

Translator: Ben Armour

2005

他是第13亿名中国公民

中国第13亿名公民于今日零时2分诞生于北京妇产医院，至此，中国人口已达13亿。小公民为男性，体重3660克、身长52厘米。其父母均为北京人。多年来，中国实施计划生育政策，有效地控制了人口过快增长，使世界60亿人口日和中国13亿人口日的到来各推迟了4年。

He is China's 1.3 Billionth Citizen

The 1.3 billionth Chinese citizen was born at Beijing Maternity Hospital at 00:02, marking the moment that China's population hit the 1.3 billion mark. The citizen is a baby boy, 52 cm long, weighing 3,600 grams. His parents are both natives of Beijing. Thanks to the Chinese compulsory family planning policy, not only has the birthrate dropped substantially, but the date when the world's population hit 6 billion and China's population reached 1.3 billion was delayed by 4 years.

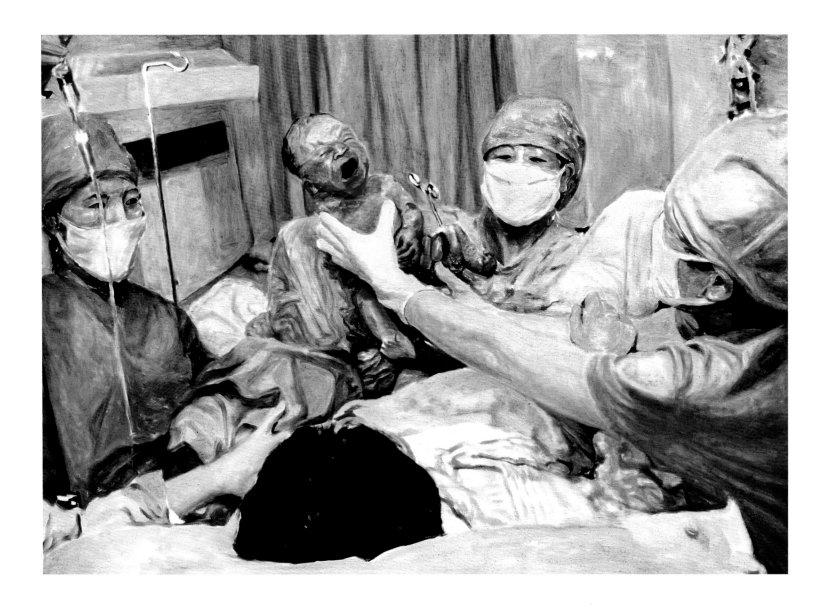

05.01.06

抗议日本"接管"钓鱼岛灯塔

昨日上午11时，日本驻华大使馆门前，一名中国人手持专门制作的汽车名片抗议日本政府"接管"钓鱼岛灯塔。50多名抗议者宣读并向日本驻华大使馆递交了抗议信，随后呼喊保钓口号，高唱国歌离去。据了解，上海、广州、长沙、重庆、香港、台湾以及美国纽约昨日也同步举行了类似抗议活动。此前，日本政府曾宣布接替日本"青年社"在中国领土钓鱼岛非法建立灯塔，企图将非法占领转为合法管理。

Chinese Protest Japan's Claim on Diaoyu Island

Yesterday at 11 am, in front of the entrance to the Japanese embassy, a Chinese person protested against the Japanese government's takeover of the Diaoyu Island lighthouse by displaying a custom-made sign while hanging out of a car. Over 50 protesters read aloud their diplomatic letter of protest and handed it to the Japanese embassy. They shouted slogans about "protecting Diaoyu Island" and sang the Chinese national anthem before eventually leaving. Similar activities were also reportedly held in Shanghai, Guangzhou, Changsha, Chongqing, Hong Kong, Taiwan and New York. Prior to this, the Japanese government had announced its plan to takeover its rule from the Japan Youth Association in an attempt to transform their detinue into a valid sovereignty by illegally maintaining a lighthouse on Diaoyu Island.

05.02.16

05.05.20

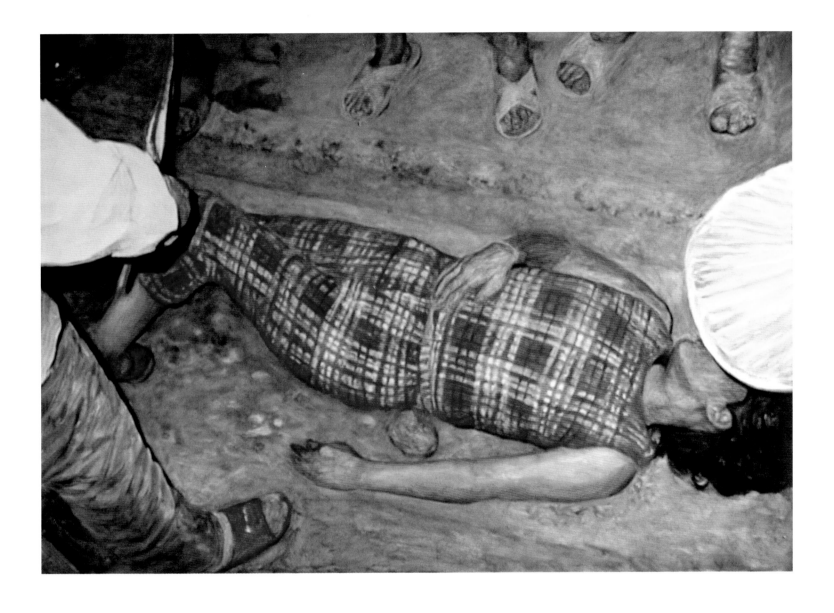

05.07.01

05.09.11

"2005"

05.01.04

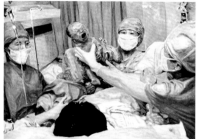

05.01.06

05.01.19

05.01.26

05.04.13

05.04.14

05.04.25

05.04.30

05.06.17

05.06.20

05.06.26

05.06.28

05.09.12

05.09.14

05.09.30

05.10.07

05.01.30

05.02.02

05.02.16

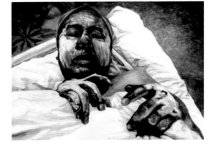

05.02.17

05.05.13

05.05.19

05.05.20

05.05.21

05.06.30

05.07.01

05.07.03

05.07.06

05.10.17

05.10.19

05.11.14

05.11.27

05.11.14

     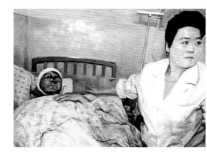  

.02.20   05.03.17   05.03.20   05.03.23   05.03.24   05.03.27   05.03.31   05.04.05

05.23   05.05.24   05.06.05   05.06.09   05.06.10   05.06.11   05.06.13   05.06.14

07.17   05.08.02   05.08.13   05.08.22   05.08.24   05.08.27   05.09.09   05.09.11

2.09   05.12.10   05.12.14   05.12.16

系列作品60幅
布面油画
每幅 70 × 100 cm
2006

Series of 60 paintings
oil on canvas
70 × 100 cm each
2006

2006

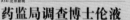

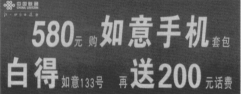

牡丹江水源疑遭污染

黑龙江牡丹江市水源地取水口发现不明絮状物，饮用水出现异味。昨日，牡丹江市政府新闻发言人通报称，造成污染的是生长在海浪河的水生生物。为保证水质，自来水公司已经加氯消毒。目前，该市市区尚未停水。

The Purification Plant in Mudanjiang City Suspected of Being Polluted

The drinking water in Mudanjiang City was found to contain some unknown materials and had a bad odor. The government of Mudanjiang City announced that the pollution was caused by some organisms in the Hailang River. To improve the drinking water quality, the wastewater treatment plant has already disinfected the water. Mudanjiang City has never stopped providing water.

06.02.22

断电救人

昨日，救援人员在50米高空架滑轮营救一爬塔女子。当日6时许，该女子爬上丰台区丽泽桥一座高压线铁塔，并停留3个多小时。受其影响，当地交通受阻三个多小时，丰益桥、丽泽桥附近地区断电。

Electrical Power Cut Off / Life Saved

Yesterday, rescue teams saved a woman from a 50-meter high tower in Lizeqiao, Fengtai District. The woman, who had climbed up the high voltage tower, was trapped for more than 3 hours. Local traffic was blocked for 3 hours, and electricity in the area near Fenyiqiao and Lizeqiao was cut off.

06.04.26

06.07.30

06.08.09

06.11.17

1.29 06.02.14 06.02.16 06.02.22 06.02.26 06.03.08 06.03.17 06.03.24

05.06 06.05.09 06.05.12 06.05.24 06.06.02 06.06.07 06.06.09 06.06.11

.08.13 06.08.17 06.08.18 06.08.19 06.08.22 06.08.27 06.08.31 06.09.03

.11.17 06.11.22 06.11.25 06.11.26 06.11.28 06.11.30 06.12.01 06.12.05

06.12.28

"2006"

06.03.26　　06.03.28　　06.04.02　　06.04.07　　06.04.13　　06.04.22　　06.04.23　　06.04.26

06.06.20　　06.06.23　　06.06.28　　06.07.13　　06.07.25　　06.07.30　　06.08.06　　06.08.09

06.09.16　　06.09.21　　06.10.08　　06.10.18　　06.10.19　　06.10.26　　06.10.29　　06.11.10

06.12.06　　06.12.09　　06.12.15　　06.12.20　　06.12.22　　06.12.27　　06.12.28

系列作品63幅
布面油画
每幅 70 × 100 cm
2007

Series of 63 paintings
oil on canvas
70 × 100 cm each
2007

2007

新京报

2007年1月7日 星期日 农历丙戌年十一月十九   今日40版 零售价1.00元

THE BEIJING NEWS

胡锦涛：全力营救被绑工人

尼日利亚警方承诺尽快查明被绑者下落；在尼被绑5工人均系四川人 *A05*

缆车故障20余人困半空

两小时后被救下，事发延庆石京龙滑雪场，遇险者包括数名外国人 *A08*

庙会黄金位
拍出5.16万

龙潭庙会小吃摊位
拍出历史最高价

京城冬泳赛"福娃"抢镜

昨日，头戴2008年奥运会吉祥物等奥运标志的女子冬泳队在进行冬泳表演。当日，北京市第二十九届冬泳表演赛在京郊延庆夏都公园举行，来自北京各界的30支代表队300多名冬泳爱好者参加了冬泳表演。据了解，北京现在有上万名冬泳爱好者。
本报记者 郭铁流 摄影报道

东单一酒楼
爆炸10人伤

A06

厨房燃气泄漏引发
事故，酒楼被停业整顿

无安全措施
矿工可停工

A08

北京下发国有煤矿
管理指导意见

日本拟再提
"入常"方案

A17

日媒体称提案要求
安理会增2-3个常任国

哥高官遭绑
6年后逃脱

从林亡命5天后获救，为哥伦比亚前
经济发展部长 *A17*

积水潭分院
明年底建成

回龙观居民将受益；北京21委办局
"一把手"将做客城市管理广播 *A08*

沪看守所长
受贿被刑拘

A14

被受贿正戴亲属嘱
赂49万元，为周提供方便

A叠(24版)/评论、时事新闻、体育新闻、文娱新闻   B叠(16版)/地球周刊

本报热线 *63190000*

京城冬泳赛"福娃"抢镜

昨日，头戴2008年奥运会吉祥物等奥运标志的女子冬泳队在进行冬泳表演。当日，北京市第二十九届冬泳表演赛在京郊延庆夏都公园举行，来自北京各界的30支代表队300多名冬泳爱好者参加了冬泳表演。据了解，北京现在有上万名冬泳爱好者。

Beijing Winter Swimming Competition Fuwa [Felicity Dolls] Attractive for Camera Shooting

Yesterday, the female Olympic Winter Swimming Team was wearing Fuwa (the mascots of the 2008 Summer Olympics in Beijing) while performing their winter swim. On the same day, Beijing's 29th Winter Swimming Performance and Competition took place in Yanqing Summer Park; 30 teams and over 300 winter swimming enthusiasts participated in the performances. According to the report, there are more than 10,000 winter swimming enthusiasts in Beijing.

07.01.07

火烧违建自称"拆得彻底"

执法队清拆违建的火焰仍在燃烧，一个孩子在曾经的家中拿出水瓢灭火。

Fire Used to "Completely Destroy" Illegal Buildings

Illegally built houses destroyed by a law enforcement team were still burning as a child with a ladle tried to put out the flames of a former home.

07.09.02

07.04.17

07.08.27

07.10.18

07.01.03 07.01.07 07.01.11 07.01.12 07.01.19 07.01.20 07.02.03 07.02.10

07.04.13 07.04.14 07.04.17 07.04.19 07.04.21 07.04.22 07.05.04 07.05.09

.06.25 07.07.05 07.07.25 07.08.15 07.08.25 07.08.27 07.08.31 07.09.02

11.14 07.11.23 07.11.27 07.11.29 07.12.05 07.12.15 07.12.16 07.12.17

07.12.22

"2007"

2008

垃圾覆麦田居民喊可惜

一车建筑垃圾倒入麦田，旁边有人对司机收费。昨日，海淀区上庄乡一处麦田，上千亩地被围，有渣土车前来倾倒建筑垃圾。麦田中有多处宽约十米的"建筑垃圾带"，垃圾堆有1米多高。附近居民认为，麦田内正长着绿油油的小麦，被垃圾埋了太可惜。对于倾倒垃圾的原因，收费人员称是为了开发盖房。

Residents Bemoan Dumpage on Crops

A driver dumped an entire truckload of construction waste onto an area of wheat fields, paying charges to someone on the site. Yesterday, there were many trucks dumping waste on over 150 acres of wheat fields located in Shangzhuang Village, Haidian District, resulting in many 'waste belts' approximately 10 meters wide and 1 meter high. Village dwellers were unhappy to witness the well-tended wheat being covered by dumped waste. A person who was receiving the fees on site said the dumping was the result of real estate development happening in that area.

08.04.12

全国哀悼3日

5月16日晚，四川竹市汉旺镇东汽中学发掘现场，一名死难学生被挖出时，手里紧紧攥着一支笔。

National Mourning for Three Days

On the evening of May 16th, during the ongoing excavation at the Dongqi Middle School, Hanwang Township, Mianzhu City, Sichuan Province, a student killed by the earthquake was pulled from the rubble, still holding a pen firmly in hand.

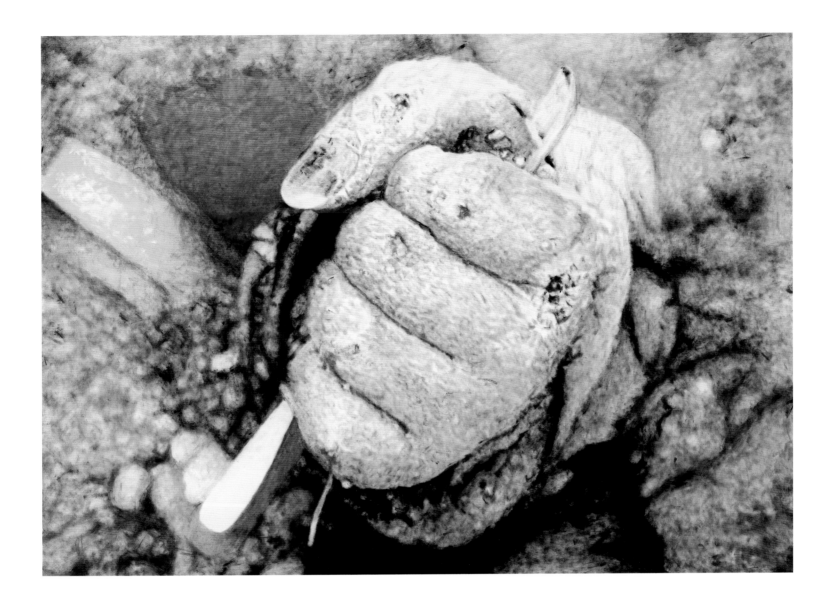

08.05.19

08.03.09

08.09.24

①女童（圆圈中左）带着白衣男子走向厕所。

②不到一分钟，女童跑向父母所在的包房。

③女童父母带着两个孩子寻找白衣男子。

④交涉时，白衣男子（圆圈中右）推搡女童父亲。

08.11.01

01.01   08.01.30   08.02.05   08.02.22   08.03.03   08.03.04   08.03.05   08.03.06

04.12   08.04.14   08.05.05   08.05.09   08.05.16   08.05.19   08.05.26   08.05.28

09.04   08.09.05   08.09.22   08.09.24   08.09.29   08.10.12   08.10.13   08.10.14

11.19   08.11.19a   08.11.26   08.11.28   08.11.29   08.12.06   08.12.08   08.12.18

08.12.08

"2008"

03.07

08.03.08

08.03.09

08.03.10

08.03.17

08.03.18

08.03.19

08.03.22

06.21

08.07.04

08.07.11

08.07.26

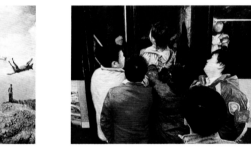

08.08.04

08.08.24

08.09.01

08.09.02

10.14a

08.10.15

08.10.17

08.10.25

08.10.26

08.10.31

08.11.01

08.11.03

3.12.29

08.12.30

系列作品58幅
布面油画
每幅140×200 cm
2009

Series of 58 paintings
oil on canvas
140×200 cm each
2009

2009

石家庄否认抵押政府大楼

当地政府称曾帮三鹿协调资金赔付，相关资金将在企业破产中清偿

三声巨响震动重庆城

巨响来历不明，手机一度打不通；有关部门否定地震说法

新长征集团原董事长受审

王妙兴涉贪超亿元；曾任上海普陀区长征镇镇长

职工用"热得快"引发火灾

安徽长丰县政府招待所两职工涉嫌犯罪被拘

嘉宾合影
累煞学生

考研试题"答案"公开叫卖

山西部分校园内该种广告泛滥；招考中心提醒作弊将被重点打击

乘客通宵排队买火车票死亡

杭州火车站称，乘客因病死亡并非排队猝死

波音 737 开进校园

嘉宾合影 累煞学生

台上站着准备合影的嘉宾，后面是学生用手或身体支撑台子。2009中国数学奥林匹克暨第24届全国中学生数学冬令营1月8日在海南琼海开营。在当天的活动中，一些嘉宾需要站在搭起来的台子上合影，为了合影嘉宾站立安全，嘉积中学学生用人体支撑台子。

Group Photo with Guests Exhausts Students

On a temporarily constructed platform, sundry guests gathered for a group photo. Behind them, many students used their hands and bodies to support the platform. The 24th National Middle School Mathematics Winter Camp for the 2009 China Mathematics Olympiad (CMO) was held on January 8 in Qionghai City, Hainan Province. To support those guests who took part in a group photo during the day's program, many students from Jiaji Middle School used their bodies to uphold the temporary platform and bolster its stability.

09.01.09

封存透析机

昨日下午，工作人员将透析机搬离，患者胡爱玲站在门前落泪。当天，位于通州区宋庄镇白庙村的"自助透析室"的三台透析机，被北京市药品监督管理局通州分区拉走封存，现场药品也同时被封。通州区卫生局副局长蔡力凯表示，这一事件已上报北京市卫生局和卫生部，由上级政府部门负责与各患者原籍政府进行协调。

Sealed-Up Dialysis Machine

Yesterday afternoon, officials from the Beijing Drug Administration, Tongzhou Branch removed three dialysis machines and sealed up drugs on-site at Baimiao Village, Songzhuang Township in Tongzhou District. A nephropathy patient, He Ailin, cried in front of the door. Cai Likai, the Deputy Head of the Tongzhou Health Bureau, disclosed that the forced closure had been reported to the Ministry of Health and to the Beijing Municipal Health Bureau, which will liaise with the local government department responsible for migrant worker patients in Beijing.

09.04.03

09.04.18

09.06.24

09.07.11

01.05 09.01.07 09.01.09 09.01.12 09.01.15 09.02.03 09.02.18 09.02.21

5.10 09.05.18 09.06.02 09.06.05 09.06.09 09.06.15 09.06.20 09.06.22

.23 09.07.24 09.07.27 09.07.31 09.08.03 09.08.06 09.08.11 09.08.16

01 09.11.09 09.11.17 09.11.20 09.11.21 09.11.26 09.12.04 09.12.12

09.11.20

"2009"

.23a   09.02.23b   09.02.25   09.03.17   09.03.29   09.04.03   09.04.18   09.04.21

.06.23   09.06.24   09.06.27   09.07.01   09.07.02   09.07.09   09.07.10   09.07.11

.08.26   09.09.04   09.09.13   09.09.26   09.10.01   09.10.04   09.10.23   09.10.27

.9.12.16   09.12.17   09.12.22   09.12.25

系列作品60幅
布面油画
每幅35×50 cm
2010

Series of 60 paintings
oil on canvas
35×50 cm each
2010

2010

新京报

2010年1月13日　星期三　农历己丑年十一月廿九　　　　　　　今日96版　零售价1.00元

央行上调存款准备金率0.5%

自下周一起，系2008年6月以来首次上调，将冻结资金2964亿　　B03·经济新闻

拳打搅局者

昨日，金盏乡008艺术区，一名艺术家（右）与一名前来抢画并撕毁海报的不明身份者厮打。当日，创意正阳艺术区、008艺术区、将府艺术区等20处将被拆迁的艺术区抱团"暖冬"，艺术家用行为、装置艺术进行维权。活动中途，一些不明身份的人冲过来撕海报、作品，引发冲突，导致现场一度混乱。

本报记者 李强 摄　C10·文娱新闻

在京民工可订外地返程票

同车次购票500张可申请专列；108对返程临客车票可预订　A19·北京民生

A07·特别报道
地铁禁报理由遭三大质疑

A10·区县两会
海淀放弃四号线北延方案

A06·热点
**百度被"黑"
4小时难访问**

攻击者自称"伊朗网军"；伊朗方面称不排除有人挑拨中伊关系

A05·要闻/A34·国际新闻
**中国反导试验
不威胁航天器**

外交部称不产生滞留空间轨道碎片；各国导弹拦截技术大盘点

A21·北京社会
三环新城再发持刀抢劫案

A26·核心报道
燕山大学"高价卖地还债"

A叠(40版)/评论、时事新闻、体育新闻　　B叠(16版)/经济新闻、财经观察　　C叠(16版)/文娱新闻　　D叠(24版)/旅游公社　　　　本报热线 67106666

拳打搅局者

昨日，金盏乡008艺术区，一名艺术家（右）与一名前来抢画并撕毁海报的不明身份者厮打。当日，创意正阳艺术区、008艺术区、将府艺术区等20处将被拆迁的艺术区抱团"暖冬"，艺术家用行为、装置艺术进行维权。活动中途，一些不明身份的人冲过来撕海报、作品，引发冲突，导致现场一度混乱。

Beating Up the Troublemakers

Yesterday, an artist (on the right) fought with an anonymous person who destroyed posters and paintings at the 008 Art Village, located in Jinzhan Village. On the same day, artists from about 20 art villages, including Chuangyi, Zhengyang, 008 and Jiangfu, collectively organized the event "Warm Winter" to safeguard their legal rights and protest the villages' demolition, presenting art performances and installations. During the event, a group of unidentified persons arrived and began destroying posters and artworks, which resulted in a scene of conflict and chaos.

10.01.13

北京艾滋病例八成为性传播

五成以上为同性传播，25年来北京已累计报告8395例，艾滋病疫情整体上仍处于低流行水平

81感染者吁修改公务员体检标准

致信两部委称存在就业歧视

五成中学生恐惧艾滋病人

40余输血感染艾滋者进京维权

寻求解决病后一系列生活和就医问题

"好想有个属于自己的家"

40余输血感染艾滋者进京维权

昨日上午，来自河南的数十位艾滋病患者、感染者与媒体见面。

Over 40 Activists Infected with HIV / AIDS Via Blood Transfusion Came to Beijing.

Yesterday morning, approximately 40 HIV / AIDS-infected patients from Henan Province spoke to members of the press.

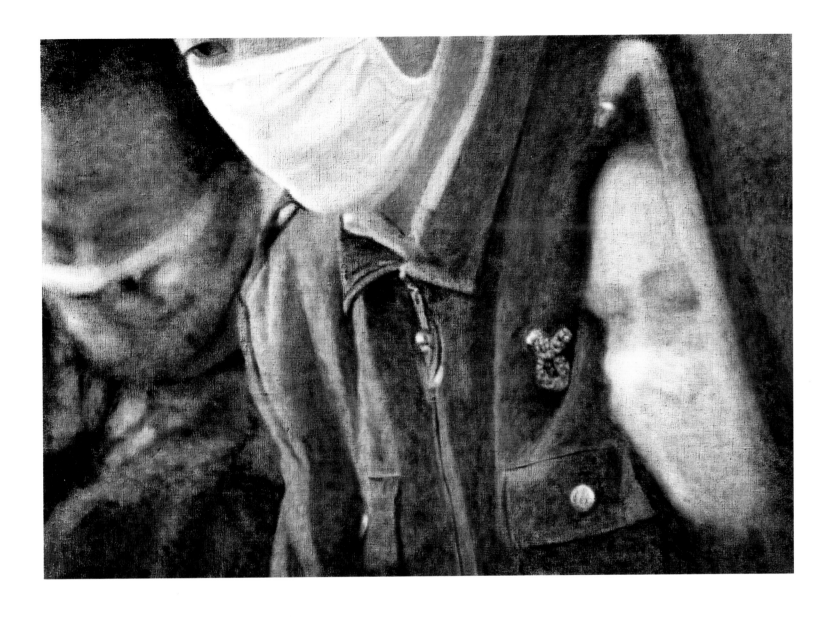

10.12.01

10.01.07

10.04.15

10.07.30

10.01.02 10.01.07 10.01.12 10.01.13 10.01.17 10.01.21 10.01.22 10.02.25

10.04.24 10.05.05 10.05.07 10.05.08 10.05.12 10.05.18 10.05.26 10.05.27

10.07.30 10.08.03 10.08.04 10.08.05 10.08.17 10.08.18 10.08.26 10.09.11

10.11.12 10.11.15 10.11.21 10.11.28 10.12.01 10.12.02 10.12.03 10.12.07

10.12.14

"2010"

   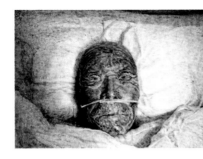    

0.03.04 10.03.25 10.03.27 10.03.30 10.04.12 10.04.15 10.04.17 10.04.23

0.05.30 10.06.01 10.06.03 10.06.09 10.06.15 10.06.28 10.07.15 10.07.28

0.09.13 10.09.14 10.10.02 10.10.22 10.10.26 10.11.02 10.11.08 10.11.11

12.14 10.12.16 10.12.22 10.12.23

系列作品60幅
布面油画
每幅 35×50 cm
2011

Series of 60 paintings
oil on canvas
35×50 cm each
2011

简历

| 1974 | 生于中国新疆石河子 |
| | 生活和工作在中国北京 |

个展

2011	"2007/2008/2009/2010", 麦勒画廊 北京-卢森, 中国北京
2008	"每日真相——夏星绘画", Morono Kiang画廊, 美国洛杉矶
	"2006", 麦勒画廊 北京-卢森, 中国北京
2007	"2005", 麦勒画廊 北京-卢森, 瑞士卢森
2006	"2004", 艺术文件仓库, 中国北京

联展

| 2003 | "质问......", 艺术文件仓库, 中国北京 |

Biography

1974   born in Shihezi, Xinjiang Province, China
           lives and works in Beijing, China

Solo Exhibitions

2011   "2007/2008/2009/2010", Galerie Urs Meile, Beijing-Lucerne, Beijing, China

2008   "Quotidian Truths: Paintings by Xia Xing", Morono Kiang Gallery, Los Angeles, USA
           "2006", Galerie Urs Meile, Beijing-Lucerne, Beijing, China

2007   "2005", Galerie Urs Meile, Beijing-Lucerne, Lucerne, Switzerland

2006   "2004", China Art Archives & Warehouse (CAAW), Beijing, China

Group Exhibition

2003   "In Search of...", China Art Archives & Warehouse (CAAW), Beijing, China

GALERIE URS **MEILE**
BEIJING · LUCERNE

麦 勒 画 廊
北 京 · 卢 森

出版: 麦勒画廊 北京-卢森

编辑: 麦勒画廊 北京-卢森
文章: 艾未未
翻译: Ben Armour (英)
设计: 李建辉
摄影: 白继开, Eric Gregory Powell

© 2011 麦勒画廊 北京-卢森, 夏星
未经出版人的书面许可,本书所有内容不可用于任何形式及目的,包括但不限于图片复印、抄录或其他信息存储及文字转换的复制及传播。
印刷: 中国北京

Publisher: Galerie Urs Meile, Beijing-Lucerne

Editor: Galerie Urs Meile, Beijing-Lucerne
Text: Ai Weiwei
Translator: Ben Armour (E)
Designer: Li Jianhui
Photography: Bai Jikai, Eric Gregory Powell

© 2011 Galerie Urs Meile, Beijing-Lucerne, Xia Xing
All rights reserved. No part of this book may be reproduced or transmitted in any form or by any means, including but not limited to photocopying, transcribing or by any information storage and retrieval system, without written permission from the publisher.
ISBN-13: 978-3-9523767-5-1

Printed in China

麦勒画廊, 北京市朝阳区草场地104号, 邮编 100015, 电话 +86 10 643 333 93
Galerie Urs Meile, No. 104, Caochangdi, Chaoyang District, Beijing, PRC 100015, T +86 10 643 333 93
Galerie Urs Meile, Rosenberghöhe 4, 6004 Lucerne, Switzerland, T +41 41 420 33 18
galerie@galerieursmeile.com, www.galerieursmeile.com